CHRISTMAS AT HOME

Country Christmas Recipes

HOLIDAY RECIPES & MORE

BARBOUR
PUBLISHING

P9-AOC-111

© 2009 by Barbour Publishing, Inc.

Compiled by Rebecca Germany.

ISBN 978-1-60260-504-6

Cover image right: Paul Poplis/Food Pix/Jupiter Images.

Published by Barbour Publishing, Inc. P.O. Box 719, Uhrichsville, Ohio 44683, www.barbourbooks.com

Our mission is to publish and distribute inspirational products offering exceptional value and biblical encouragement to the masses.

 Member of the
Evangelical Christian
Publishers Association

Printed in China.

Contents

Munchers and Sippers. 7

Bread. 26

Breakfast 40

Meats, Casseroles, and Soups 57

Vegetables, Sides, and Salads 80

Cakes, Desserts, and Pies 107

Cookies and Candies 128

Munchers and Sippers

Christmas is doing a little
something extra for someone.

CHARLES SCHULZ

Bacon Cheese Spread

1 pound round loaf bread
1 pound bacon, cooked crisp
8 ounces shredded Colby
   and/or Monterey Jack Cheese

1 cup grated Parmesan cheese
1 cup mayonnaise
1 small onion, minced

Cut top off the bread and hollow out the center, leaving a 1-inch shell. (Reserve center bread for dipping in the spread.) Mix bacon, cheeses, mayonnaise, and onion together. Spoon in to bread bowl and top with bread lid. Place on a baking sheet and bake at 350 degrees for 1 hour. Serve hot with bread, crackers, or tortilla chips.

Barbecue Bites

2 pounds smoked sausage chunks   2 cups grape jelly
   or meatballs
2 cups barbecue sauce

Combine sauce and jelly. Place meat in slow cooker and pour sauce mixture over all. Set on medium heat and stir occasionally until meat is heated through.

Black-Eyed Pea Dip

1 (16 ounce) can black-eyed peas, drained
3 green onions, chopped with tops
½ cup sour cream

1 teaspoon garlic salt
½ cup salsa
4 slices bacon, fried and
    crumbled

Place peas in a blender, reserving ⅓ cup. Process until smooth. Blend in onions, sour cream, and garlic salt. Transfer to a bowl and stir in reserved peas, salsa, and bacon. Serve with tortilla chips, bagel chips, or corn chips.

Cheddar Stuffed Mushrooms

16 ounces fresh whole mushrooms,
    cleaned
2 tablespoons minced onion

¾ cup herb stuffing mix
½ cup sharp cheddar cheese,
    shredded
¼ cup butter, melted

Remove stems from mushrooms and set caps aside. Finely chop half the stems and discard the rest. In a bowl, combine chopped mushrooms, onion, stuffing mix, cheese, and butter. Mix well. Spoon about a teaspoon of mixture into each mushroom cap. Place on a greased cookie sheet. Bake at 350 degrees for 10 to 12 minutes. Serve warm.

Chestnuts and Bacon

2 (8 ounce) cans whole water chestnuts
1 to 2 pounds bacon, strips cut in half

⅔ cup ketchup
1 cup sugar

Wrap a piece of bacon around each chestnut and secure with a toothpick. Bake at 350 degrees for 30 minutes. Drain fat. Mix ketchup and sugar together and spoon over bacon chestnuts. Bake another 30 minutes.

Dried Beef Ball

1 (8 ounce) package cream cheese,
   softened
¼ cup Parmesan cheese, grated

1 tablespoon prepared
   horseradish
1 cup dried beef, finely cut

Blend cheeses and horseradish; form into a ball. Chill overnight. Roll in beef.
Serve with assorted crackers.

Hanky Pankies

1 pound ground beef
1 pound hot Italian sausage
1 pound processed American cheese,
   diced
1 tablespoon Worcestershire sauce

1 teaspoon oregano
½ teaspoon garlic salt
Dash of pepper
   2 loaves party rye bread

Brown meats together; drain fat. Turn heat to lowest setting and add cheese to meat, stirring until melted. Add Worcestershire sauce, oregano, garlic salt, and pepper. Spoon mixture onto each slice of bread. Heat at 350 degrees for 10 to 15 minutes (or freeze in layers separated by waxed paper until needed).

Sauerkraut Balls

1½ to 2 pounds bulk sausage
2 medium onions, diced
½ cup butter
2 teaspoons black pepper
2 teaspoons salt
1 teaspoon seasoned salt
3 cups flour

1 quart chicken stock
1 pound sauerkraut
2 eggs, beaten
1 cup milk
Flour
Cracker crumbs

In a large, 4-quart pot, brown sausage and onion in butter with seasonings. Add 3 cups flour and mix well; stir in chicken stock and sauerkraut. Cook until thickened. Refrigerate 6 to 8 hours. Combine eggs and milk. Drop sauerkraut mixture by spoonfuls into flour and roll to coat, then dip into egg mixture and then into cracker crumbs. Deep fry at 350 degrees. Makes 16 dozen.

Caramel Corn

2 cups brown sugar
½ cup water
¼ cup butter

Pinch of baking soda
4 quarts popped corn

In a saucepan, cook sugar, water, and butter to the softball stage. Add baking soda. Immediately pour over popcorn. Spread out on waxed paper to cool.

Kettle Corn

⅓ cup corn oil   ½ cup popcorn kernels
½ cup sugar   Salt to taste

In a heavy 3-quart saucepan, heat the oil over medium-high heat. Test the oil's readiness with several kernels. When those pop, add the sugar and the remaining popcorn. Cover with a lid. Shake the pan over the heat while the popcorn pops. When the popping stops, remove the pan from the heat and immediately transfer to a bowl.

Oat Snack Mix

½ cup butter
⅓ cup honey
¼ cup packed brown sugar
1 teaspoon cinnamon
½ teaspoon salt

3 cups oat cereal squares
1½ cups old-fashioned oats
1 cup small pretzels
1 cup mixed nuts

In a saucepan, combine butter, honey, brown sugar, cinnamon, and salt. Heat until butter melts and stir until sugar dissolves. In a large bowl, combine cereal, oats, pretzels, and nuts. Drizzle with butter mixture and mix well. Bake in a 9 x 13-inch pan at 275 degrees for 45 minutes. Stir every 15 minutes. Makes 6 cups.

Christmas Tea

2 cups instant tea mix
¾ cup red hot candies
1 envelope lemonade drink
  flavoring

2 cups instant orange drink
  powder
1 cup sugar
½ teaspoon ground cloves

Combine all ingredients and store in an airtight container until ready to serve.
For each cup of boiling water, add 2 teaspoons of mix.

Hot Cranberry Punch

8 cups hot water
1½ cups sugar
¾ cup orange juice
¼ cup lemon juice

4 cups cranberry juice
12 whole cloves
½ cup red hot candies

In a 5-quart Crock-Pot, combine water, sugar, and juices. Stir until sugar is dissolved. Place cloves in a tea ball or cheesecloth, then place it and the candies in the Crock-Pot. Cover and cook on low for 2 to 3 hours until well heated. Remove cloves before serving. Makes 3½ quarts.

Party Punch

5 cups double-strength tea, chilled
2¼ cups sugar
2½ cups orange juice
chilled
1½ cups unsweetened grapefruit juice

⅔ cup lemon juice
¼ cup lime juice
1½ quarts ginger ale,

Combine all ingredients except for ginger ale. Cover punch and chill in refrigerator. When ready to serve, add the chilled ginger ale. Stir to blend thoroughly.

Wassail

1½ cups water
½ cup brown sugar
1 cinnamon stick
½ tablespoon whole cloves

1 gallon apple cider
1 lemon
1 orange

In a saucepan, bring water, brown sugar, cinnamon, and cloves to a boil. Pour apple cider into a Crock-Pot and add hot spice mixture. Squeeze the juice of lemon and orange into the cider. Float pieces of the peelings on top. Serve hot.

Eggnog

2 eggs
4 cups milk
1 cup sweetened condensed milk
1 teaspoon vanilla

¼ teaspoon salt
¼ teaspoon nutmeg
1 cup whipping cream

In a blender, combine eggs, milk, condensed milk, vanilla, salt, and nutmeg. In a bowl, whip the whipping cream to a peak, then fold in with the eggnog. Chill.

Frothy Chocolate

3 cups milk
1 egg, beaten
⅓ cup semi-sweet chocolate chips

1 tablespoon sugar
½ teaspoon cinnamon

In a medium saucepan, warm milk over medium-low heat until hot but not boiling. In a small microwave-safe bowl, mix together egg, chocolate chips, sugar, and cinnamon. Microwave on high for 20-second intervals, stirring in between until melted and smooth. Add chocolate to the milk and whisk together until well blended. Serve in mugs with whipped cream and chocolate sprinkles on top.

Christmas is the season for kindling the fire
of hospitality in the hall, the genial
flame of charity in the heart.

WASHINGTON IRVING

Bread

Heap on the wood!—the wind is chill;
But let it whistle as it will,
We'll keep our Christmas merry still.

SIR WALTER SCOTT

Baking Powder Biscuits

2 cups flour
2 teaspoons baking powder
½ teaspoon salt

4 tablespoons butter, lard,
   or shortening
⅔ cup milk

Sift flour once; measure and add baking powder and salt, and sift again. Cut in butter. Gradually add milk, stirring until soft dough is formed. Add a splash of milk if dough won't form. Turn out on lightly floured board and gently knead for 30 seconds, just enough to shape. The key is to not work the dough much at all. Roll to ½-inch thickness and cut with 2-inch floured biscuit cutter. Bake on ungreased sheet at 400 degrees for 12 to 15 minutes. Makes 12 biscuits.

Refrigerator Rolls

1 package quick yeast
½ cup warm water
1 teaspoon sugar
½ cup shortening
½ cup sugar

1 egg, beaten until light
2 cups lukewarm water
2 teaspoons salt
Flour

Blend yeast, ½ cup warm water, and 1 teaspoon sugar; let stand 15 to 30 minutes. Cream together sugar and shortening. Add egg, 2 cups warm water, yeast mixture, and salt. Stiffen dough by mixing in ½ cup flour at a time. Turn dough out on a board and knead as for bread. Allow to rise once in greased bowl until doubled in bulk. Work down and store in refrigerator until ready to bake (no more than 2 days). Two to three hours before serving, bring dough out and knead. Place in greased bowl and let rise until doubled in bulk. Form dough into rolls. Bake at 375 degrees for 20 minutes.

Rich Egg Rolls

2 packages yeast
½ cup warm water
1½ cups lukewarm milk
¼ cup sugar
1 teaspoon salt

3 eggs, beaten
¼ cup butter, softened
7½ cups flour
Butter, melted

Dissolve yeast in warm water; stir in milk, sugar, salt, eggs, butter, and half of the flour. Use a spoon to mix until smooth. Add enough flour to mix the dough by hand. Turn onto a lightly floured surface and knead. Let rise. Roll dough out into a large circle, spread with melted butter, cut into 12 "pizza" triangles, and roll up, starting with the larger outside edge. Let rise until doubled. Bake at 350 degrees for 12 to 15 minutes.

Pumpkin Muffins

2½ cups pureed pumpkin
4 eggs
1 cup oil
1 cup water
4 cups flour
2¾ cups sugar
1¾ teaspoons baking soda

½ teaspoon baking powder
1 tablespoon cinnamon
1 tablespoon nutmeg
1 tablespoon ground cloves
1 teaspoon salt
1¼ cups raisins
¾ cup chopped walnuts

In a large bowl, mix pumpkin, eggs, oil, and water. In another bowl, sift flour, sugar, baking soda, baking powder, cinnamon, nutmeg, cloves, and salt. Stir into pumpkin mixture. Add raisins and nuts. Line muffin tin cups with paper liners and fill each almost to the top. Bake at 375 degrees for 15 minutes. Makes 3½ dozen.

Cottage Cheese and Nut Bread

1 cup cottage cheese
1 cup chopped nuts
1 cup soft bread crumbs
2 teaspoons lemon juice
1 teaspoon salt

½ teaspoon black pepper
1 tablespoon butter
½ teaspoon minced onions
1 tablespoon water

Mix cheese, nuts, bread crumbs, lemon juice, salt, and pepper. Fry onion in butter until just browning. Remove from heat and add water. Blend onion into cheese mixture. Pour into an 8 x 8 greased baking dish and bake at 400 degrees for 25 to 30 minutes, until brown.

Hominy Bread

1 cup boiled hominy
1½ cups milk
¾ cup molasses
1 cup cornmeal
1 cup white flour

1 tablespoon baking soda
1 teaspoon baking powder
1 teaspoon salt
1 egg, beaten
1 tablespoon shortening,
  melted

In a bowl, mash hominy. Add milk and molasses to the hominy and beat together. In a separate bowl, combine cornmeal, flour, baking soda, baking powder, and salt. Slowly add mixture to the hominy. Add beaten egg and melted shortening. Place in greased loaf pan. Bake at 350 degrees for about 35 minutes.

Marmalade Bread

1¾ cups all-purpose flour
1½ teaspoons baking powder
½ teaspoon baking soda
melted
½ teaspoon salt
1 egg, beaten

¾ cup milk
⅔ cup sugar
4 tablespoons butter,

1 cup orange marmalade

Sift together flour, baking powder, baking soda, and salt into a large mixing bowl. In another bowl, mix together the egg, milk, sugar, butter, and marmalade. Pour moist mixture into the flour mixture, folding gently until combined into a batter. Don't overmix. Spoon the batter into a greased and floured loaf pan. Bake at 350 degrees for 45 to 60 minutes until lightly browned and the sides have begun to pull away slightly from the pan.

Pumpkin Bread

3 cups flour
2 teaspoons baking soda
1½ teaspoons salt
1 teaspoon cinnamon
1 teaspoon nutmeg

3 cups sugar
1 cup shortening, melted
2 cups pureed pumpkin
4 eggs
⅔ cup water

In a large bowl, sift together flour, baking soda, salt, cinnamon, nutmeg, and sugar. Combine shortening, pumpkin, eggs, and water; add to dry ingredients, blending well. Bake at 350 degrees for 1 hour. Cool completely before slicing.

Pumpkin Cornbread

1½ cups cornmeal
½ cup whole wheat flour
1 tablespoon baking powder
3 tablespoons sugar
1 teaspoon cinnamon

1 teaspoon salt
1 egg, beaten
3 tablespoons oil
¾ cup pureed pumpkin
1½ cups milk

In a large bowl, sift dry ingredients. In a separate bowl, blend egg, oil, pumpkin, and milk. Combine with dry ingredients. Pour into a greased 8 x 8 pan. Bake at 350 degrees for 30 to 35 minutes.

Date Nut Bread

1 cup chopped dates
2 teaspoons baking soda
1 cup boiling water
1¾ cups flour
1 teaspoon baking powder
½ teaspoon salt

2 teaspoons butter, softened
1 cup sugar
1 egg
1 teaspoon vanilla
1 cup chopped nuts

Bring water to boil and add chopped dates; sprinkle baking soda on dates. It should foam. Remove from heat and let stand 15 minutes. In a small bowl, sift together flour, baking powder, and salt. In a separate bowl, cream together butter and sugar, then beat in egg and vanilla. In a large bowl, alternate combining dry ingredients, date mixture, and creamed mixture. Fold in nuts. Pour into 2 greased loaf pans. Bake at 325 degrees for 1 hour and 15 minutes. Bread will freeze well.

Honey Apple Raisin Nut Bread

1 cup honey
½ cup shortening
2 eggs, beaten
2 cups flour
¼ teaspoon salt
1 teaspoon baking soda
½ teaspoon cinnamon

⅛ teaspoon ground allspice
⅛ teaspoon ground cloves
1 cup applesauce
1 cup oatmeal
1 cup nuts, chopped
1 cup raisins

In a large mixing bowl, blend honey and shortening; mix in eggs and beat until fluffy and light. In a separate bowl, sift together flour, salt, baking soda, cinnamon, allspice, and cloves. Add dry mixture to the honey mixture, alternating with applesauce. Stir in oatmeal, nuts, and raisins. Pour into a greased loaf pan and bake at 325 degrees for 1 hour.

Poppy Seed Bread

3 cups flour
2¼ cups sugar
1½ cups milk
1⅛ cups oil
3 eggs

1½ teaspoons poppy seeds
1½ teaspoons salt
1½ teaspoons baking powder
1½ teaspoons almond flavoring
1½ teaspoons butter flavoring

Mix all ingredients. Pour into 2 greased bread pans. Bake for 1 hour at 350 degrees. Cool for 5 to 10 minutes and remove from pans.

Glaze:
¾ cup sugar
¼ cup orange juice
½ teaspoon butter flavoring

½ teaspoon vanilla
½ teaspoon almond flavoring

Mix and pour over hot bread.

Christmas Eve was a night of song that wrapped itself about you like a shawl. But it warmed more than your body. It warmed your heart. . .filled it, too, with melody that would last forever.

BESS STREETER ALDRICH

Breakfast

Christmas hath a beauty. . .
lovelier than the world can show.

CHRISTINA G. ROSSETTI

Cinnamon Sticky Buns

2 loaves frozen bread dough, thawed
1 cup pecans, chopped
1 cup butter
1 cup brown sugar

1 (5.1 ounce) package cooked
    vanilla pudding
2 teaspoons cinnamon
2 tablespoons milk

Let bread dough rise. Grease a large cake pan with butter and cover the bottom with chopped pecans. Roll pieces of dough into 1-inch balls and place on top of the nuts. Combine butter, brown sugar, pudding, cinnamon, and milk. Spread the mixture over the dough. Cover with plastic wrap. Let the rolls rise in the refrigerator overnight. Bake at 350 degrees for 30 minutes. Invert onto a platter to serve.

Cinnamon Coffee Cake

1½ cups flour
½ cup sugar
2½ teaspoons baking powder
½ teaspoon salt
¼ cup oil
1 egg

¾ cup milk
½ cup brown sugar
2 tablespoons flour
2 tablespoons oil
2 teaspoons cinnamon

Sift together flour, sugar, baking powder, and salt. In a separate bowl, combine ¼ cup oil, egg, and milk; blend into dry mixture for batter. In a dry bowl, combine brown sugar, flour, 2 tablespoons oil, and cinnamon. Pour half of batter in a greased 8 x 8 pan. Top with half of the cinnamon-sugar mixture. Add remaining batter and top with remaining cinnamon-sugar mixture. Bake at 350 degrees for 20 to 25 minutes.

Apple Pancakes

2 eggs
2 cups flour, sifted
1 cup milk
1 cup applesauce

1 teaspoon salt
2 tablespoons baking
  powder
4 tablespoons butter, melted

Combine all ingredients, mixing until smooth. Cook on a hot griddle or skillet.
Serve with Apple Cider Syrup (see p. 44). Makes about 16 pancakes. Serves 4.

Apple Cider Syrup

2 cups apple cider
1 cup sugar
2 tablespoons cornstarch

1 teaspoon cinnamon
2 tablespoons fresh lemon juice
4 tablespoons butter

In a saucepan over medium heat, combine all ingredients except butter, heating until mixture thickens. Boil for 1 minute. Remove from heat and stir in the butter. Serve hot over pancakes.

Swedish Oven Pancakes

½ cup butter
4 eggs
1 teaspoon salt

4 cups milk
2 cups flour

Heat oven to 400 degrees and place butter in a 9 x 13-inch pan to melt in the oven. Mix all other ingredients together and pour into the hot buttered pan. Bake for 35 to 40 minutes or until set. Serve with syrup.

Dutch Honey

1 cup light corn syrup

1 cup sugar

1 cup whipping cream

1 teaspoon vanilla

Cook syrup and sugar together until it will string. In a separate small saucepan, heat cream until hot but not boiling. Let both cool awhile, then stir together with vanilla. Serve with pancakes.

Breakfast Casserole

6 to 8 slices bread,
    broken in small pieces
1 pound sausage,
    cooked and crumbled
1 cup cheddar cheese,
    shredded

6 to 8 eggs
2 cups milk
1 teaspoon mustard
¼ teaspoon salt

Grease a 9 x 13-inch pan and place bread crumbs in bottom. Sprinkle sausage and cheese over the bread. In a large bowl, beat eggs and milk until fluffy, and add mustard and salt. Pour over the bread, sausage, and cheese. Can be refrigerated overnight. Bake at 350 degrees for 45 minutes.

Makes 8 servings.

Cornmeal Mush

2¾ cups water
1 cup yellow cornmeal
1 cup cold water

1 teaspoon salt
1 teaspoon sugar

Bring 2¾ cups water to a boil. Combine the remaining ingredients and add to boiling water, stirring constantly. Cook until thick over medium heat, stirring frequently. Cover pot and continue cooking 10 to 15 minutes over low heat. At this point, you can serve the hot mush with a topping of fried sausage and onions and a bit of butter. Otherwise, pour hot mush into a lightly greased loaf pan and refrigerate for several hours. Turn out of pan and cut into ½-inch slices. Deep fry in oil until golden brown. Serve with butter and syrup.

Deluxe Grits

4 cups water
1 cup old-fashioned grits
¼ cup butter
1 teaspoon salt

2 cups cheddar cheese, shredded
6 to 8 slices bacon
4 eggs
1 cup milk

In a 3-quart saucepan, bring water, grits, butter, and salt to a boil. Reduce heat to simmer for 10 minutes. Stir in cheese until it melts. Allow grits to continue to simmer while frying bacon in a skillet until crisp. Drain bacon on a paper towel, then crumble into grits. In a small bowl, beat eggs with milk. Remove grits from heat and fully combine with eggs. Pour mixture into a well-greased 9 x 13-inch pan. Bake at 350 degrees for 20 to 30 minutes. Makes 8 servings.

Baked Millet Cereal

1 cup uncooked millet
1½ cups milk
4 cups hot water

⅔ cup chopped raisins
½ cup unsweetened coconut
1 teaspoon vanilla

Combine all ingredients and pour into a lightly greased 9 x 13-inch baking dish.
Bake at 350 degrees for 30 minutes, then remove and stir. Return cereal to oven
and bake another 30 minutes. Serve hot. Makes 8 servings.

Baked Oatmeal

1 cup sugar
½ cup oil
2 eggs
2 teaspoons baking powder

3 cups quick oatmeal
1 cup milk
¾ cup coconut
¼ cup pecans, chopped

Mix all ingredients and pour into a lightly greased 8 x 8 baking pan. Bake at 350 degrees for 30 minutes.

Creamed Eggs and Biscuits

6 tablespoons butter
6 tablespoons flour
1½ teaspoons salt
Dash of black pepper

3 cups milk
6 hard-boiled eggs, chopped
Ham or bacon, chopped

In a saucepan, melt butter and stir in flour, salt, and pepper until well blended. Slowly add milk and stir constantly. Cook until smooth. Add eggs and ham. Serve over toast or biscuits. Makes 6 servings.

Scotch Eggs

4 hard-boiled eggs, peeled   ½ cup bread crumbs
1 pound Italian pork or turkey sausage   Oil

Divide the sausage into fourths. Mold sausage around each hard-boiled egg, coating evenly. If needed, dampen the sausage with some water, then roll the sausage in bread crumbs. Deep fry in hot oil till sausage is brown and crisp. Drain well before serving.

Sausage Balls

1 pound sausage
2 cups all purpose baking mix

8 ounces cheddar cheese,
grated

Combine all ingredients. Roll into small balls and place on a cookie sheet. Bake at 350 for 10 to 15 minutes.

Bacon Gravy

2 to 4 slices bacon,
    cut into small pieces
1/3 cup flour
1/2 teaspoon salt

1/8 teaspoon black pepper
1 teaspoon sugar
3 cups milk

Fry bacon over medium heat until crisp. Stir in the flour until grease is absorbed. Season with salt, pepper, and sugar. Slowly add milk with a whisk, stirring until it reaches a boil. Boil for 5 minutes until thick. Serve over biscuits, toast, or potatoes.

My idea of Christmas, whether old-fashioned or modern, is very simple: loving others. Come to think of it, why do we have to wait for Christmas to do that?

BOB HOPE

Meats, Casseroles, and Soups

Christmas is not a time nor a season,
but a state of mind. To cherish peace
and goodwill, to be plenteous in mercy,
is to have the real spirit of Christmas.

CALVIN COOLIDGE

Barbecued Chipped Ham

1½ pounds chipped ham   1 tablespoon vinegar
1 cup ketchup   1 onion, minced
3 tablespoons brown sugar

Mix all ingredients and simmer in a large saucepan for 30 minutes, stirring often.
Serve over buns.

Black-Eyed Peas and Ham

2 ham hocks or a ham bone
   with ham left on it
1 pound dried black-eyed peas
1 medium onion, chopped

1 clove garlic, minced
Pepper
Salt

Rinse and sort peas. Place the ham hocks, peas, onion, and garlic in a Crock-Pot and cover completely with water. Cook 8 to 10 hours on low, or 4 to 5 hours on high. Check occasionally. You may need to add more water if peas start to look dry. Don't let peas turn to mush. Season with salt and pepper to taste.

Ham Balls

1 pound ground ham
1 pound ground pork
2 eggs, beaten
1 cup dried bread crumbs
1⅓ cups milk

1 teaspoon dry mustard
1 cup crushed pineapple
½ cup brown sugar
2 tablespoons vinegar

Mix ground ham and pork, eggs, bread crumbs, and milk. Roll into 1½-inch balls; place in a 9 x 13-inch pan. Mix mustard, pineapple, brown sugar, and vinegar. Pour over ham balls. Bake at 325 degrees for 1 hour.

Ham-Cranberry Loaf

2 eggs, beaten
¾ cup milk
1 teaspoon salt
⅛ teaspoon pepper
¼ teaspoon ground cloves

1 cup bread crumbs
1 pound ground uncooked
   ham
1 pound ground lean pork
1 cup whole cranberry sauce

Mix eggs, milk, salt, pepper, cloves, and bread crumbs; let stand a few minutes until crumbs are soaked in. Add ham and pork, mixing well with hands. Place in shallow baking dish, shaping into a loaf. Spread cranberry sauce over top of loaf. Bake at 400 degrees for 1 hour.

Ham and Turnip Bake

5 cups turnips, diced
2 cups cooked ground ham
  (or turkey, chicken, or beef)
1 cup onion, minced
1 cup celery, minced
½ cup green pepper, minced

1 egg
3 tablespoons butter, melted
½ cup soft bread crumbs
Salt
Pepper
1 cup processed American
  cheese, grated

Cook diced turnips in boiling water for about 15 minutes or until tender; drain and mash. Add ham, onion, celery, green pepper, egg, butter, and bread crumbs. Season to taste with salt and pepper. Pour into lightly greased Crock-Pot. Cover and cook on high setting for 2 to 4 hours or on low setting for 4 to 8 hours. Before serving, sprinkle with grated cheese.

Huntington Chicken

4 cups chicken broth
8 tablespoons flour
½ pound processed cheese, grated
1 (4 to 5 pound) whole chicken,
   stewed and boned

2 cups macaroni (measured
   after cooking)
Salt and pepper to taste
7 slices bread, crumbled
¼ cup butter, melted

In a large saucepan, heat broth. Take a cup of broth and blend with flour to make a paste. Add to pan of broth to create a gravy. Stir in cheese until melted. Add chicken and macaroni. Place in ungreased 9 x 13 baking dish. Combine bread with butter and cover casserole. Bake at 350 degrees for 45 minutes, or until bubbly. (Casserole may be frozen without topping prior to baking.)

Lamb Stew

1 pound lamb, cut into ¾-inch pieces
2 tablespoons olive oil
3 cups beef broth
3 cloves garlic, minced
1 teaspoon ground marjoram
1 bay leaf
¼ teaspoon salt
¼ teaspoon black pepper

2 large potatoes, peeled and
    cut into ½-inch chunks
1½ cups carrots, sliced
1½ cups celery, chopped
½ cup onion, chopped
½ cup sour cream
3 tablespoons flour

In a large soup pot, brown meat in oil; drain excess fat. Add broth, garlic, marjoram, bay leaf, salt, and pepper and bring to a boil. Reduce heat, cover, and simmer for 20 minutes until meat is rather tender. Add potatoes, carrots, celery, and onion. Bring to a boil again and then reduce heat, cover, and simmer for 30 minutes until vegetables are tender. Remove bay leaf. In a bowl, blend sour cream and flour, then stir in ½ cup of the liquid from the stew. Add sour cream mixture to the stew and cook until thickened.

Home-Style Turkey

1 (12 to 14 pound) whole turkey
6 tablespoons butter, divided
4 cups warm water
3 tablespoons chicken bouillon

2 tablespoons dried minced
onion
2 tablespoons dried parsley
2 tablespoons seasoning salt

Rinse turkey and remove giblet packet from inside. Put turkey on a rack in a roasting pan. Cut approximately 6 pockets into the skin over each breast and insert approximately 1 tablespoon butter in each pocket. In a bowl, dissolve bouillon in water; add onion and parsley. Pour over turkey. Sprinkle seasoning salt all over turkey. Cover the turkey with foil and bake at 350 degrees for 3 hours; remove foil. Bake another 30 to 60 minutes. Insert a thermometer to check that meat has reached 180 degrees. Remove and let rest 15 minutes before carving.

Savory Crock-Pot Turkey

1 (6 to 7 pound) turkey breast
    on bone, thawed
½ cup onion, chopped
½ cup celery, chopped
1 bay leaf

1 teaspoon chicken bouillon
    granules
½ cup water
1 teaspoon salt
½ teaspoon black pepper

Clean out turkey breast cavity and fill with onion, celery, and bay leaf. Place turkey in 5- to 6-quart Crock-Pot. Mix bouillon granules and water until granules are dissolved; pour over turkey. Sprinkle turkey with salt and pepper. Cover and cook on low for 8 to 9 hours or until juice of turkey no longer runs pink when center is cut. Remove bay leaf. Refrigerate turkey up to 4 days or freeze up to 4 months.

Giblet Gravy

Turkey liver, gizzard, heart,
    neck, and wing tips
1 teaspoon salt, divided
3 hard-boiled eggs, peeled
    and sliced thin

¾ cup prepared cornbread
    dressing
4 cups milk
Black pepper

In a saucepan, place turkey giblets and cover with water. Add ½ teaspoon salt. Bring to a boil and cook until meat is tender. Drain, reserve the broth in the saucepan, and discard bones. Chop the meat and place in broth; boil. Add eggs, dressing, milk, ½ teaspoon salt, and pepper to taste.

Turkey Rice Casserole

¼ cup butter, melted
1 cup raw long grain rice
½ cup onion, chopped
2¼ cups chicken broth
½ cup green pepper, chopped
½ cup celery, chopped

1½ cups turkey or ham, cubed
1 (6.5 ounce) can sliced
  mushrooms, drained
Cheddar or American cheese,
  shredded

In a large frying pan, melt butter then add rice and onion while stirring. Add broth. Cover pan and cook for 10 to 15 minutes. Add green pepper and celery, and cook another 10 minutes or until rice is tender. Stir occasionally. Mix in turkey and mushrooms. Pour into a 2-quart baking dish with lid and bake covered at 350 degrees for 15 to 20 minutes. In last 5 minutes of baking, sprinkle with a layer of cheese. Return to oven until cheese melts. Makes 5 to 6 servings.

Day After Casserole

1 sweet onion, sliced
2 cups broccoli, chopped
2 carrots, peeled and sliced
1 to 1½ cups leftover turkey
   or chicken, chopped

1 can cream of chicken soup
1 cup sour cream
2 to 3 cups leftover
   stuffing/dressing

Boil onion, broccoli, and carrots in a small amount of water for 5 minutes, then drain. Combine vegetables with meat, soup, and sour cream; pour into a casserole dish and top with stuffing. Bake at 350 degrees for 20 to 25 minutes until bubbly.

Hot Chicken Salad

2 cups cooked chicken or turkey,
   chopped
1 cup bread cubes
1 cup celery, chopped
2 tablespoons minced onion
½ cup sliced almonds, toasted

½ teaspoon salt
1 cup mayonnaise
2 tablespoons lemon juice
1 cup cheddar cheese,
   shredded
1 cup crushed potato chips

Mix chicken, bread, celery, onion, almonds, and salt. Place in a 9 x 13-inch pan. In a bowl, blend mayonnaise and lemon juice. Spread on top of chicken mixture. Sprinkle with cheese and chips. Bake at 450 degrees for 15 to 20 minutes.

Venison Roast

1 (3 to 5 pound) venison roast
¼ teaspoon pepper
¼ teaspoon salt
¼ cup oil
2 cans cream of mushroom soup

1 envelope dry onion soup mix
1½ cups water
1 (6.5 ounce) can
    mushrooms, drained
2 cloves garlic, minced

Sprinkle pepper and salt on meat. In a skillet, brown all sides of roast in oil. Combine soups and water; add mushrooms and garlic; pour over roast. Set Crock-Pot temperature on low and cook approximately 6 hours or until meat easily pulls apart. Or bake in a Dutch oven at 375 degrees for 3 to 4 hours.

Pheasant with Wild Rice Stuffing

3 pounds cleaned pheasant
2 tablespoons butter
¾ cup celery, diced
¼ cup onion, diced

1 cup mushrooms,
    thinly sliced
1 teaspoon salt
¼ teaspoon pepper

1 tablespoon dried parsley
½ teaspoon dried rosemary
1½ cups cooked wild rice
3 bacon slices

Rinse pheasant; pat dry. Melt butter in a frying pan. Add celery, onion, and mushrooms. Sauté until vegetables are tender and translucent. Remove from heat. Add remaining ingredients, except the bacon, tossing with a fork. Spoon stuffing into the cavity of the bird and truss the bird by tying a piece of string to the end of the neck skin and pulling it over the back. Slip the ends of the wings over the back and press them close to the body. Press the thighs close to the body and draw ends of the string back on each side and up over the thighs. Cross the string between the legs and tie it down under the tail. Place bird on a rack in shallow roasting pan. Lay bacon slices over the top of the breast. Roast at 325 degrees for 2 hours, basting occasionally with pan drippings. Remove string before cutting and serving. Makes 3 to 4 servings.

Supreme Baked Macaroni and Cheese

2 cups small curd cottage cheese
1 cup sour cream
1 egg, beaten
½ teaspoon salt
½ teaspoon garlic salt

Dash of pepper
2 cups cheddar cheese
7 ounces elbow macaroni,
   cooked and drained
Paprika

Combine cottage cheese, sour cream, egg, salt, garlic salt, and pepper. Fold in cheese and macaroni and stir until well coated. Pour into a greased 2-quart baking dish. Bake at 350 degrees for 25 to 30 minutes. Sprinkle with paprika. Makes 8 servings.

Chestnut and Butternut Squash Soup

4 celery stalks, chopped
4 leeks, chopped
2 teaspoons oil
5½ cups chicken broth, divided
2½ cups butternut squash,
   cooked and pureed

1½ cups chestnuts,
   cooked and peeled
2 tablespoons fresh ginger, minced
1 teaspoon dried thyme
2 teaspoons mace
1⅓ cups sour cream

In a 3-quart saucepan over medium heat, sauté the celery and leeks in the oil and ½ cup of the broth until the vegetables are soft and translucent, 8 to 10 minutes. Stir in the squash, chestnuts, ginger, thyme, and mace. Transfer the mixture to a food processor and process until smooth. Return the mixture to the pan. Stir in the remaining 5 cups broth. Bring to a boil over high heat, then reduce the heat to medium-low and simmer for 7 minutes. Season to taste with the pepper. Serve topped with sour cream.

Lentil Pottage

2 tablespoons oil
1 large onion, chopped
4 stalks celery, chopped
2 tablespoons garlic, minced

2 quarts water
1½ cups dry lentils
4 to 6 chicken bouillon cubes
Salt and pepper to taste

In a large saucepan, heat oil and sauté onion, celery, and garlic until the onion is translucent. Add water, lentils, and bouillon and bring to a boil. Reduce heat to a simmer for 45 minutes. Lentils should be tender. Season to taste.

Peanut Butter Soup

1 cup peanut butter
3 cups milk, divided
½ cup celery, chopped
1½ cups water

1 potato, grated
2 teaspoons salt
½ teaspoon black pepper

Mix the peanut butter with 1 cup milk, and heat 2 cups milk in a double boiler. In a saucepan, cook the celery in water until tender. Add grated potato to the celery and cook; stir mixture until thickened. Add hot milk to cooked vegetables, then blend in peanut butter mixture, salt, and pepper. Beat with mixer to cream the soup. Serve hot.

Split Pea Soup

2⅓ cups dried green split peas
6 cups chicken or vegetable stock
2 tablespoons butter
1 medium onion, chopped
1 stalk celery, chopped

1 carrot, chopped
1 small potato, diced
1 clove garlic, minced
1 teaspoon salt

Wash and sort peas. Combine all ingredients in a large stockpot. Bring to a boil, then cover and simmer over low heat for 2 to 3 hours, stirring occasionally. Puree all or part of the soup in a blender or food processor before serving. Consider adding cooked turkey or chicken to the finished soup.

Turkey Bone Soup

Bones and trimmings from one
   roasted turkey
6 cups water
3 teaspoons chicken bouillon
1½ teaspoons salt
¼ teaspoon ground sage

1 bay leaf
3 medium carrots, sliced
2 stalks celery, sliced
2 medium onions, chopped
½ cup rice or 1 cup
   dried noodles
2 tablespoons parsley

In a large pot, put the turkey bones in water and add bouillon, salt, sage, and bay leaf. Cover and simmer for 1½ hours. Remove bones. Add carrots, celery, onion, and rice. Cover and simmer for 30 minutes. Garnish with parsley. Makes 6 to 8 servings.

May we not "spend" Christmas or "observe" Christmas, but rather "keep" it.

PETER MARSHALL

Vegetables, Sides, and Salads

Christmas, my child, is love in action.
Every time we love, every time
we give, it's Christmas.

DALE EVANS ROGERS

Acorn Squash Rings

1 acorn squash
¼ cup butter, melted
½ cup whole cranberries (or dried)
¼ cup brown sugar, packed

½ cup apple, finely chopped
1 teaspoon cornstarch
2 teaspoons cold water

Cut the unpeeled whole squash into ¼-inch rings with very sharp knife. Remove and discard seeds. Place rings in a shallow baking dish and set aside. In a bowl, blend butter, cranberries, brown sugar, and apples. Bake squash at 400 degrees for 20 minutes, or until skin loosens and can be removed easily. Spoon sugared fruit mixture into each ring. Bake another 10 to 15 minutes, or until tender. Spoon juice from baking dish into a small saucepan. Dissolve cornstarch in cold water and whisk into juice. Cook over medium heat until thickened. Pour over rings.

Stuffed Acorn Squash

2 medium acorn squash
Water
½ pound Italian turkey
    or pork sausage
½ pound lean ground beef

1½ teaspoons salt
½ teaspoon cinnamon
2 cups tart apples, chopped
¼ cup raisins
Salt

4 tablespoons brown
    sugar, packed
2 tablespoons butter,
    melted

Cut each of the squash in half; remove the seeds. Place the squash, cut sides down, in an ungreased baking pan. Then add water to the depth of ¼-inch and bake, uncovered, until the squash is tender, at 400 degrees for 30 to 40 minutes. While the squash is baking, brown the meat in a large skillet; drain off fat. Remove the skillet from the heat and season with 1½ teaspoons salt and the cinnamon. Mix apples and raisins in with the meat. When the squash are cooked, place them on a plate, cut side up. Drain off remaining liquid from the baking dish, rinse, and dry. Scoop the pulp from the acorn squash, leaving a shell that is at least ¼-inch thick. Season the shells with salt to taste. Mash the pulp and mix into the meat mixture. Spoon the mixture into the shells, piling them full, and sprinkle with 1 tablespoon brown sugar on each. Drizzle with the melted butter. Bake uncovered until the apple is tender, about 20 to 30 minutes. Serve hot.

Amish Turnips

2 cups cooked turnips
⅔ cup bread crumbs, divided
1 egg
2 tablespoons brown sugar

1 cup milk
Salt and pepper to taste
1 tablespoon butter

Cook turnips until tender, drain cooking water, and mash turnips. Add ½ cup bread crumbs to turnips, saving remainder for top. Mix in egg, sugar, milk, and salt and pepper. Pour into a greased baking dish. Dot with butter and remaining crumbs. Bake at 375 degrees for 45 minutes.

Baked Corn

¼ cup butter, melted
1 small box cornbread mix
1 can creamed corn

1 can whole kernel corn, drained
2 eggs, beaten
3 tablespoons milk

In a mixing bowl, blend butter with cornbread mix. Add corn, eggs, and milk. Pour into a greased baking dish. Bake at 400 degrees for 30 minutes.

Baked Yams and Apples

2 medium-sized Southern yams
   or sweet potatoes*
½ cup brown sugar, packed
⅓ cup pecans, chopped
½ teaspoon cinnamon

½ teaspoon ginger
2 apples, peeled, cored,
   quartered, and sliced
¼ cup butter

Bake yams in microwave for 5 minutes on high, until just fork tender. Peel yams and cut into 1-inch slices. In a bowl, blend brown sugar, pecans, cinnamon, and ginger; toss apples in the mixture. Alternate layers of apple mixture and yams in 9 x 9 baking dish. Dot top with butter. Bake at 350 degrees for 35 to 40 minutes.

* Or use 2 (16 ounce) cans cooked sweet potatoes and skip the cooking step.

Gingered Spaghetti Squash

1 small spaghetti squash, halved
    with seeds removed
2 tablespoons butter

1 tablespoon honey
½ tablespoon minced ginger
Salt and black pepper

Place squash on baking dish and add the butter, honey, and ginger. Season to taste with salt and pepper. Bake at 375 degrees for 45 to 60 minutes until squash is slightly tender. Do not overcook. Spoon out squash and serve warm.

Honey-Ginger Carrots

2 pounds carrots, scraped
   and sliced diagonally
½ cup golden raisins
½ cup butter, melted

6 tablespoons honey
2 tablespoons lemon juice
½ teaspoon ginger
½ cup almonds, toasted

Cook carrots in a small amount of boiling water for 8 minutes; drain. Combine carrots, raisins, butter, honey, lemon juice, and ginger. Spoon into an ungreased 1-quart baking dish. Bake uncovered at 375 degrees for 30 to 35 minutes or until carrots are tender. Sprinkle with almonds. Makes 8 servings.

Maple-Glazed Parsnips

⅓ cup real maple syrup
¼ teaspoon prepared mustard
2 teaspoons butter
5½ cups parsnips,
    diagonally sliced (¼-inch)

3 tablespoons water
¼ teaspoon salt
Dash of black pepper
2 teaspoons dried parsley

In a small bowl, combine maple syrup and mustard; stir well and set aside. In a large nonstick skillet, melt butter over medium heat. Add parsnips, water, salt, and pepper; cover, reduce heat to medium-low, and cook 12 minutes or until tender, stirring occasionally. Add syrup mixture; cook, uncovered, over medium-high heat 1 minute or until lightly glazed, stirring constantly. Remove from heat; sprinkle with parsley.

Potato Bake

10 potatoes, cooked and cubed
4 slices bread, cubed
1 onion, chopped
1 cup butter, melted

2 tablespoons dried parsley
½ cup cheese, grated
¾ cup milk
1 cup crushed potato chips

Combine all ingredients except potato chips and pour into an ungreased 8 x 8-inch baking pan. Top with chips. Bake at 325 degrees for 1 hour.

Sloppy Potatoes

3 medium potatoes, sliced
1 medium onion, sliced
1 tablespoon butter

½ teaspoon salt

In a medium saucepan, bring all ingredients to a boil. Reduce to low and cook 15 minutes, stirring occasionally.

Sweet Potato Casserole

2 cups cooked sweet potatoes,
    mashed (1 large can drained)
½ teaspoon salt
¼ cup butter
½ cup milk
1 cup sugar

2 eggs, beaten
1 teaspoon vanilla
1 cup brown sugar
⅓ cup flour
½ cup butter, melted
1 cup pecans, chopped

Mix sweet potatoes, salt, butter, milk, sugar, eggs, and vanilla. Pour into a greased 8 x 8 baking dish. In a bowl, mix brown sugar, flour, butter, and pecans. Spread over sweet potato mixture. Bake at 350 degrees for 35 minutes.

Stewed Tomatoes

1 quart canned tomatoes
1 teaspoon salt
¼ cup sugar
1 tablespoon butter

2 tablespoons flour
½ cup milk
Soda crackers or bread

In a medium saucepan, cook tomatoes with salt for 15 minutes. Add sugar and butter. In a small bowl, slowly combine flour and milk until there are no lumps. Add floury milk to tomatoes, stirring over heat until thickened. To serve, break up crackers or bread in serving dish and pour tomatoes over them. Stir and serve.

Amish Dressing

8 tablespoons butter, divided
1 loaf stale bread, cubed
½ cup carrot, shredded
1 cup celery, finely chopped
¼ cup onion, finely chopped
6 eggs, well beaten
2 cups milk

1 cup boiled potatoes, chopped
2 cups chicken broth with
    shredded chicken
2 teaspoons chicken soup base
Salt and black pepper

Melt 4 tablespoons butter in a large frying pan; toss bread in butter until toasted. Set aside. In frying pan, melt remaining 4 tablespoons butter and sauté carrots, celery, and onion until tender. Combine bread, sautéed vegetables, eggs, milk, potatoes, broth, and soup base. Season to taste with salt and pepper. Pour into a baking pan and bake at 325 degrees for 45 minutes.

Chestnut Turkey Stuffing

1 pound chestnuts
1 medium onion, chopped
3 stalks celery (or heart of 1 bunch),
    chopped
1 loaf stale bread, crumbled

2 tablespoons dried parsley
1 teaspoon oregano
Salt and pepper to taste
2 eggs, beaten
½ cup butter, melted

Pierce chestnuts with a sharp knife, then steam for 20 minutes to make them easier to shell. Shell and chop them coarsely. In large bowl, lightly toss chestnuts, onion, celery, bread, parsley, oregano, salt, and pepper. Add eggs and butter; toss well. If too dry, add little sprinkles of water. More bread can be added to the stuffing if more volume is needed. Fill large cavity and neck cavity of turkey and fasten shut with steel skewers. Roast as directed for your turkey.

Sausage-Cornbread Dressing

1 pound ground pork sausage
2 medium onions, chopped
4 stalks celery, chopped
6 cups crumbled cornbread
   (approximately an 8 x 8-inch loaf)
3 cups dry bread cubes

1 cup pecans, toasted and
   coarsely chopped
2 teaspoons sage
¼ teaspoon salt
1 teaspoon pepper
4 cups turkey broth
2 large eggs, beaten

In a large skillet, brown sausage, onion, and celery; cook over medium heat, stirring until sausage crumbles. Drain well. In a large bowl, combine cornbread, bread, pecans, sage, salt, and pepper; then add sausage mixture. Add broth and eggs, stirring well. Spoon into a lightly greased 9 x 13-inch baking dish. Bake at 350 degrees for 45 minutes or until browned.

Noodles

3 eggs
3 cups flour
3 teaspoons salt

¾ cups milk
3 teaspoons baking powder

Mix all ingredients together and shape into a ball. If mixture is sticky, add more flour. If too dry to form a ball, add more milk. Once in a ball, knead with hands. Spread flour on a flat surface and flatten ball of dough with heel of hands, then roll with a rolling pin to desired thickness. Spread flour on dough and turn dough over and flour that side. Use a pizza cutter to cut noodles to desired width. Coat noodles with more flour and allow to air dry for 4 to 6 hours. Shake off excess flour. Store in a paper bag for a couple of days or freeze in a plastic bag. Cook in boiling water or broth for 10 minutes (approximately 20 if frozen).

Apple-Cabbage Slaw

3 cups cabbage, shredded
2 cups apples, thinly sliced
1½ teaspoons lemon juice
½ cup sour cream or plain yogurt
2 teaspoons honey

1 tablespoon vinegar
½ teaspoon prepared mustard
½ teaspoon salt
¼ teaspoon pepper

In a large bowl, combine cabbage and apples; sprinkle with lemon juice. In a small bowl, mix together sour cream, honey, vinegar, mustard, salt, and pepper. Pour dressing over cabbage and apples; toss to coat.

Apple Tree Salad

2 cups apples, chopped
1 cup raisins
1 cup celery, diced
⅓ cup pecans or walnuts, chopped

Combine all ingredients. Serve.

½ cup mayonnaise
1 tablespoon sugar (optional)
Pinch of cinnamon

Carrot Salad

1½ pounds carrots, cut diagonally
1 (10 ounce) can tomato soup
    concentrate
1 medium onion, chopped
½ teaspoon salt

½ teaspoon pepper
1 tablespoon prepared mustard
½ cup sugar
½ cup oil
¼ cup vinegar

Cook carrot slices in water until just tender. Mix soup, onion, salt, pepper, mustard, sugar, oil, and vinegar; add carrots. Marinate overnight.

Christmas Salad

1 (3 ounce) package strawberry
    gelatin dessert
1 (15 ounce) can whole cranberry sauce
1 (3 ounce) package lemon gelatin
    dessert
1 ounce cream cheese
1 (8 ounce) can crushed pineapple,
    undrained

¼ cup walnuts, chopped
1 (3 ounce) package lime
    gelatin dessert
1 (8 ounce) can pears with juice,
    chopped
1½ cups water, divided

In a bowl, dissolve strawberry gelatin in ¼ cup hot water. Add cranberry sauce and pour into a 2-quart glass dish. Chill until set. In a mixing bowl, dissolve lemon gelatin in ¼ cup hot water. Beat cream cheese until smooth then mix into lemon gelatin. Combine crushed pineapple and its juice with walnuts and add to lemon mixture. Pour on top of strawberry layer. Chill until set. In another bowl, dissolve lime gelatin in 1 cup boiling water. Add pears with juice and pour on top of lemon layer. Chill until firm.

Cinnamon Cherry Salad

1 cup boiling water
¼ cup red hot cinnamon candies
1 (3 ounce) package cherry gelatin

1 cup cold water
1 cup applesauce

Bring water to a boil. Turn to low and dissolve candies, stirring constantly. Stir in gelatin until dissolved. Pour into glass dish. Add cold water and applesauce. Chill until set.

Cranberry Salad

1 (20 ounce) can crushed pineapple
2 (3 ounce) packages cherry
    gelatin dessert
1 cup boiling water
1 (15 ounce) can whole cranberry
    sauce

3 tablespoons lemon juice
1 teaspoon grated lemon peel
½ teaspoon nutmeg
2 cups sour cream
½ cup pecans, chopped

Drain pineapple and reserve juice. Dissolve gelatin in water and add pineapple juice. Wait until cooled, then add cranberry sauce, lemon juice, lemon peel, and nutmeg. Chill until thickened. Fold in pineapple, sour cream, and pecans. Makes 8 to 10 servings.

Cranberry and Walnut Coleslaw

2 cups red cabbage, finely sliced
2 cups green cabbage, finely sliced
¼ cup red onion, thinly sliced
1 cup dried cranberries
1 cup walnuts, coarsely chopped

⅓ cup apple cider vinegar
⅓ cup oil
⅓ cup sugar
1 teaspoon celery seed

In a large bowl, toss together cabbage, onion, cranberries, and walnuts. In a separate bowl, combine vinegar, oil, sugar, and celery seed. Coat cabbage mixture with dressing. Chill for 3 hours. Stir and drain off excess liquid before serving.

Ribbon Salad

2 (3 ounce) packages lime
   gelatin dessert
5 cups hot water, divided
4 cups cold water, divided
1 (3 ounce) package lemon
gelatin dessert
8 ounces cream cheese

4 ounces miniature
   marshmallows
½ cup crushed pineapple,
   drained
1 cup whipped topping
2 (3 ounce) packages cherry
   gelatin dessert

In a bowl, dissolve lime gelatin in 2 cups hot water and add 2 cups cold water. Pour into a 9 x 13-inch pan and chill until set. In a bowl, dissolve lemon gelatin in 1 cup hot water, then add cream cheese and marshmallows. When lemon mixture starts to set, add pineapple and whipped topping. Pour over first layer and chill until set. In a bowl, dissolve cherry gelatin in 2 cups hot water and add 2 cups cold water. Chill until cherry mixture starts to set, then pour over second salad layer. Chill all until firm.

Sauerkraut Salad

1 bag sauerkraut
1 to 2 medium red apples
⅓ cup oil

3 to 5 tablespoons sugar
Pinch of salt
Black pepper to taste
(optional)

Drain and squeeze out excess juice from sauerkraut. Core and grate apples with peels on. Stir sauerkraut and apples together. In a small bowl, blend oil, sugar, salt, and pepper; pour over sauerkraut.

Christmas is not just a time for festivity and merry making. It is more than that. It is a time for the contemplation of eternal things. The Christmas spirit is a spirit of giving and forgiving.

J. C. PENNEY

Cakes, Desserts, and Pies

Christmas waves a magic wand over
this world, and behold, everything
is softer and more beautiful.

NORMAN VINCENT PEALE

Beet Cake

1 (16 ounce) can beets, drained
½ cup applesauce
½ cup oil
3 eggs
2 cups sugar

2 cups flour
½ cup cocoa
1 teaspoon baking soda
½ teaspoon salt

In a blender, puree beets, applesauce, oil, and eggs. Add sugar slowly on low speed. In a large mixing bowl, sift together flour, cocoa, baking soda, and salt. Add beet mixture to dry mixture and mix well. Bake in a greased and floured 9 x 13-inch pan at 350 degrees for 40 to 45 minutes.

Chocolate Kraut Cake

½ cup well-drained sauerkraut
⅔ cup shortening
1½ cups sugar
3 eggs
1 teaspoon vanilla
2¼ cups flour

½ cup cocoa powder
1 teaspoon baking soda
1 teaspoon baking powder
¼ teaspoon salt
1 cup water
Chopped nuts (optional)

Chop sauerkraut very tiny; set aside. In a large bowl, cream shortening and sugar. Beat in eggs, one at a time. Add vanilla. In a separate bowl, blend flour, cocoa powder, baking soda, baking powder, and salt. Add to creamed mixture alternately with the water. Stir in chopped kraut. Add nuts. Pour into a greased 9 x 13-inch pan and bake at 375 degrees for 35 minutes.

Root Beer Cake

1 cup sugar
2 cups flour
½ cup butter
1 tablespoon baking powder

½ teaspoon vanilla
2 eggs
1 teaspoon salt
⅔ cup root beer

Combine all ingredients. Blend with mixer at low speed and beat 3 minutes at medium speed. Pour into a greased 9 x 13-inch baking pan and bake at 375 degrees for 30 to 35 minutes.

Gingerbread

½ cup shortening	2¼ cups sifted flour	2 cups sugar
2 tablespoons sugar	1 teaspoon baking soda	4 tablespoons cornstarch
1 egg	½ teaspoon salt	4 cups boiling water
1 cup molasses	1 teaspoon ginger	½ cup butter
1 cup boiling water	1 teaspoon cinnamon	4 teaspoons vanilla

In a large bowl, blend shortening, 2 tablespoons sugar, and egg. Beat in molasses and 1 cup boiling water. In a separate bowl, sift together flour, baking soda, salt, ginger, and cinnamon and beat into shortening mixture until smooth. Pour into a well-greased and floured 9 x 9-inch pan. Bake at 325 degrees for 45 to 50 minutes. Serve hot with vanilla sauce made by placing 2 cups sugar and cornstarch in a saucepan and slowly adding 4 cups boiling water. Boil, stirring constantly, until thickened. Add butter and vanilla.

Apple Betty

4 cups apples, peeled and sliced
¼ cup water
1¾ teaspoons cinnamon
4 teaspoons brown sugar

½ cup oatmeal
1 tablespoon butter
2 tablespoons brown sugar

Mix together apples, water, cinnamon, and 4 teaspoons brown sugar. Pour into a greased 8 x 8-inch pan. In a separate bowl, blend oatmeal, butter, and 2 tablespoons brown sugar. Sprinkle over top of apple mixture. Bake at 375 degrees for 30 minutes.

Caramel Dumplings

1½ cups flour
½ cup sugar
2 tablespoons shortening,
   softened
⅔ cup milk

⅛ teaspoon salt
2 teaspoons baking soda
1½ cups water
1½ cups brown sugar
2 tablespoons butter

In a bowl, combine flour, sugar, shortening, milk, salt, and baking soda; set aside. In a large saucepan, blend water, brown sugar, and butter; bring to a boil. Drop dumpling mixture into boiling syrup by the spoonful. Cover and boil slowly for 15 minutes without removing lid. Serve warm.

Brownie Pudding

1 cup sifted flour
1½ cups sugar
2 tablespoons cocoa
2 teaspoons baking powder
½ teaspoon salt
½ cup milk
2 tablespoons oil

1 teaspoon vanilla
½ cup chocolate chips
¾ cup nuts, chopped
1 cup brown sugar
¼ cup cocoa
1 cup hot water

In a large bowl, combine flour, white sugar, 2 tablespoons cocoa, baking powder, and salt. Add milk, oil, and vanilla. Beat until smooth. Add chocolate chips and nuts. Pour into greased 8 x 8-inch pan. Mix brown sugar and ¼ cup cocoa; sprinkle over batter. Pour hot water over all. Bake at 350 degrees for 45 minutes.

Date Pudding

4 cups brown sugar, divided
3½ cups water
2 tablespoons butter
1 cup dates, chopped

1 cup nuts, chopped
1 cup sweet milk
2 cups flour, sifted
4 teaspoons baking powder

In a saucepan, bring 3 cups brown sugar, water, and butter to a boil to create a syrup. In a separate bowl, mix 1 cup brown sugar with dates, nuts, milk, flour, and baking powder. Pour syrup into bottom of 9 x 13-inch greased cake pan. Drop dough by teaspoonfuls into the syrup. Bake at 350 degrees for 45 to 60 minutes. Serve warm with whipped cream.

Indian Pudding

3 cups milk
⅓ cup cornmeal
¼ cup molasses
¼ cup sugar

½ teaspoon salt
½ teaspoon ginger
½ teaspoon cinnamon
Butter

In a large saucepan, cook milk over medium heat until bubbles form at edges. Slowly stir cornmeal and molasses into milk. Continue to cook and stir until thickened. After about 10 minutes, remove from heat and add sugar, salt, ginger, and cinnamon. Pour into an 8 x 8-inch baking dish that has been greased with butter. Bake at 275 degrees for 2 hours, until set. Serve with whipped cream.

Ozark Pudding

2 eggs
1 teaspoon baking powder
1½ cups sugar
½ cup flour

1 teaspoon salt
1 teaspoon vanilla
2 cups apples, diced
1 cup nuts, chopped

In a large bowl, beat eggs; add dry ingredients. Fold in apples and nuts. Spread in greased 8 x 8-inch pan. Bake at 375 degrees for 50 to 60 minutes. Serve warm with whipped cream or ice cream. Makes 9 servings.

Rice Pudding

2 cups water
Pinch of salt
1 cup uncooked rice
5 cups milk
5 eggs, beaten

1 cup sugar
2 teaspoons vanilla
1 cup raisins
Cinnamon

In a large saucepan, boil water with salt. Add rice and cook over medium heat until water is absorbed (approximately 20 minutes for white rice). Add milk and cook until thick, stirring occasionally. Remove from heat. Combine eggs, sugar, and vanilla. Blend egg mixture with rice mixture, fold in raisins, and pour into a casserole dish. Sprinkle the top with cinnamon and bake at 350 degrees for 45 minutes.

Old-Fashioned Mincemeat

4 pounds apples, peeled, cored,
   and chopped
1 pound ground beef or minced
   stew meat, cooked till tender
1 pound raisins

3 cups water, divided
2 cups brown sugar
3 teaspoons cinnamon
   (or more to taste)
½ teaspoon nutmeg

Grind apples. In a saucepan, cook apples with meat until apples are saucy. In another saucepan, cook raisins until soft in 1 cup water with brown sugar, cinnamon, and nutmeg. Add raisins to apple mixture, including 2 cups of water. Simmer all for 1 hour. Makes 6 pints that can be used immediately in pies or canned for later use.

Pumpkin Crunch

3 eggs, beaten
1½ cups sugar
12 ounces pureed pumpkin
1½ cups evaporated milk
4 teaspoons pumpkin spice

½ teaspoon salt
1 box yellow cake mix
1 cup butter, melted
1 cup nuts, chopped

In a bowl, mix the first 6 ingredients well. Pour into a lightly greased cake pan. Sprinkle cake mix over the top, drizzle with butter, and sprinkle with nuts. Bake at 350 degrees for 40 minutes. Serve with whipped cream.

Pumpkin Dessert

¾ cup sugar
½ teaspoon salt
1 teaspoon cinnamon
½ teaspoon ginger
¼ teaspoon ground cloves
2 large eggs, beaten

1 (15 ounce) can pumpkin
   puree
¼ cup all purpose baking mix
1 (12 ounce) can evaporated
   milk

In a large mixing bowl, mix sugar, salt, cinnamon, ginger, and cloves. Add eggs to sugar mixture, then blend in pumpkin. Dissolve the baking mix in a bit of the milk, then add to the pumpkin mixture. Gradually stir in the milk. Pour into a lightly greased 8 x 8-inch baking dish. Sprinkle additional cinnamon lightly over the top. Bake for 15 minutes at 425 degrees. Reduce heat to 350 degrees and bake 40 to 50 minutes or until a knife inserted in the middle comes out clean. Cool and serve with whipped topping or ice cream.

Fried Apples with Nuts

4 apples
2 tablespoons butter
1 tablespoon oil

½ cup walnut or pecan halves
  or pieces
3 tablespoons brown sugar
  or maple syrup

Halve and core the apples but don't peel them. Slice about ¼-inch thick. Heat a big frying pan over medium heat and add the butter and oil. Add the apples and cook, stirring often, until just starting to soften—about 10 minutes. Don't let them brown too much. While doing that, toast the nuts in a dry frying pan over medium heat or in the oven until lightly toasted. Stir often so they don't burn. Add the toasted nuts to apples, as well as the brown sugar. Stir well and reduce heat to low, cooking until apples are tender. Serve with ice cream.

Brown Sugar Pie

1 cup brown sugar
3 tablespoons flour
Pinch of salt
1 unbaked 8-inch pie shell

1 (12 ounce) can evaporated
milk
2½ tablespoons butter
Cinnamon

In a bowl, blend brown sugar, flour, and salt. Cover the bottom of the pie shell with the mixture. Pour the evaporated milk over the top of that, but do not stir or mix in. Dot with butter and sprinkle liberally with cinnamon. Bake at 350 degrees for 50 minutes, or until the filling just bubbles up in the middle. The filling will not completely set, but that is fine. Serve at room temperature but store in the refrigerator.

Butternut Squash Pie

1 cup evaporated milk
1½ cups cooked butternut
   squash, mashed
½ cup sugar
1 tablespoon flour
½ teaspoon salt

½ teaspoon ginger
½ teaspoon nutmeg
½ teaspoon cinnamon
2 large eggs
1 unbaked 9-inch pie shell

Heat milk and squash together in double boiler. In a mixing bowl, mix sugar, flour, salt, ginger, nutmeg, and cinnamon. Add eggs. Beat well with beaters or whisk. Add mixture to milk and squash in double boiler. Stir together well. Heat but do not boil. Pour warm filling into pie shell. Bake at 400 degrees for 10 minutes, then reduce heat to 350 degrees. Bake until pie sets, about 15 to 20 minutes. Top with whipped cream to serve.

Eggnog Pie

1 teaspoon unflavored gelatin
1 tablespoon cold water
1 cup milk
½ cup sugar
2 tablespoons cornstarch
½ teaspoon salt

3 egg yolks, beaten
1 tablespoon butter
1 tablespoon vanilla
1 cup whipping cream,
   whipped to a peak
1 (9-inch) baked pie shell

Soak gelatin in cold water. In a large saucepan, scald milk. In a bowl, combine sugar, cornstarch, and salt; mix well. Add to scalded milk and cook until thick. Add eggs and cook 2 minutes. Add gelatin, butter, and vanilla. Cool, then fold in whipped cream. Pour into a baked pie shell. Can be topped with fruit.

Mock Pecan Pie

½ cup sugar
¼ cup butter, melted
1 teaspoon vanilla
¼ teaspoon salt

3 eggs
1 cup corn syrup
1 cup oatmeal
1 (9-inch) unbaked pie shell

In a large bowl, blend sugar and butter; add vanilla and salt. Whip in eggs, then add corn syrup. Stir in oatmeal. Pour into an unbaked pie shell and bake at 350 degrees for 35 to 40 minutes, or until the center is almost set.

Unless we make Christmas an occasion to share our blessings, all the snow in Alaska won't make it "white."

BING CROSBY

Cookies and Candies

It is good to be children sometimes, and never better than at Christmas, when its mighty Founder was a child Himself.

CHARLES DICKENS

Bessie's Sugar Cookies

3 eggs, beaten
2 teaspoons vanilla
2 cups sugar
1 cup lard or shortening

1 cup milk
½ teaspoon baking soda
7 cups flour (approximately)
4 teaspoons baking powder

In a large bowl, mix eggs, vanilla, sugar, and lard until smooth. In a separate bowl, blend milk and baking soda together; add to egg mixture. In another bowl, sift together flour and baking powder, then slowly add to egg mixture until dough is the right texture for handling. Roll dough out on a floured surface and cut into shapes with cookie cutters. Bake at 350 degrees for 10 minutes.

Cherry Nut Cookies

1 cup butter, softened
2 cups brown sugar
2 eggs
2 teaspoons vanilla
4 cups flour

1 teaspoon baking soda
½ teaspoon salt
1 cup walnuts, chopped
½ cup maraschino cherries,
    chopped

In a large bowl, cream together butter and sugar. Add eggs and vanilla; beat until smooth. Blend in flour, baking soda, and salt. Add walnuts and cherries. Form into 2 long rolls, 2 inches thick. Wrap in waxed paper and chill. Cut into ¼-inch slices and bake at 375 degrees for 8 to 10 minutes until lightly browned.

Chocolate Cookies

1½ cups sugar
½ cup shortening
3 eggs
2 cups flour

½ teaspoon baking soda
½ teaspoon salt
½ cup cocoa powder

In a large mixing bowl, cream sugar and shortening. Add eggs, then sift in dry ingredients. Chill. Shape into balls. Roll in powdered sugar. Bake at 350 degrees for 8 to 10 minutes.

Chocolate Cottage Cheese Cookies

1½ cups shortening
3½ cups sugar
4 eggs
4 teaspoons vanilla
2 cups cottage cheese
1 cup cocoa powder
2 teaspoons baking powder

1 teaspoon salt
1 teaspoon baking soda
5½ cups flour
1 cup chopped nuts and/or
    chocolate chips
Powdered sugar

In a large bowl, cream shortening, sugar, eggs, and vanilla. Add cottage cheese, cocoa powder, baking powder, salt, and baking soda. Slowly mix in flour. Fold in nuts and/or chips. Shape dough into balls and roll in powdered sugar. Bake at 350 degrees for 10 to 15 minutes.

Date Nut Pinwheels

1 cup brown sugar
1 cup sugar
1 cup butter, softened
3 eggs
4 cups flour
1 teaspoon baking soda

1 teaspoon baking powder
½ cup sugar
½ cup water
1 pound dates, chopped fine
1 cup walnuts, chopped

In a large bowl, cream together brown sugar and 1 cup sugar with butter. Add eggs and beat well. In a separate bowl, sift together flour, baking soda, and baking powder, then blend in with creamed mixture. Chill. Roll out to ¼-inch thickness. Prepare filling by combining ½ cup white sugar and water in a saucepan. Add dates and boil over low heat until thick, stirring constantly. Cool. Add nuts. Makes 7½ dozen.

Frosted Drop Cookies

½ cup shortening
1½ cups brown sugar
1 teaspoon vanilla
2 eggs
2½ cups flour

1 teaspoon baking soda
½ teaspoon baking powder
½ teaspoon salt
1 cup sour cream
½ cup walnuts, chopped

In a large bowl, thoroughly cream shortening, sugar, and vanilla. Beat in eggs. In a separate bowl, sift together dry ingredients and add to shortening mixture alternately with sour cream. Stir in nuts. Drop by teaspoonfuls onto greased cookie sheet. Bake at 350 degrees for 10 to 12 minutes. Frost with butter icing.

Butter Icing

6 tablespoons butter
2 cups powdered sugar

1 teaspoon vanilla
Hot water

In a saucepan, heat butter until golden brown. Remove from heat and beat in powdered sugar and vanilla. Add enough hot water until the mixture is spreading consistency.

Maple Nut Cookies

½ cup brown sugar
½ cup butter-flavored shortening
1 egg
1¾ cups flour
¼ teaspoon soda
¼ teaspoon salt

¼ teaspoon maple flavoring
¼ teaspoon vanilla
2 cups walnuts, chopped
1 cup powdered sugar
2 tablespoons milk
1/2 teaspoon maple flavoring

In a large bowl, cream brown sugar and shortening. Beat in egg. In a separate bowl, combine dry ingredients and add to sugar mixture. Stir in flavoring and nuts. Drop by teaspoonfuls onto greased cookie sheet. Bake at 350 degrees for 10 to 12 minutes. Make a glaze by blending powdered sugar, milk, and maple flavoring. Drizzle over top of cooled cookies. Makes 2 dozen.

Raisin Nut Drops

2 cups raisins	1 teaspoon vanilla
1 cup water	4 cups flour
1 teaspoon baking soda	1 teaspoon baking powder
1½ cups sugar	1 teaspoon cinnamon
1 cup shortening	1 teaspoon nutmeg
3 eggs	1 cup walnuts, chopped

In a saucepan, boil raisins in water for 5 minutes. Allow to cool, then stir in baking soda. In a separate bowl, cream together sugar and shortening. Beat in eggs and vanilla. Combine sugar mixture with raisin mixture. In a separate bowl, sift together flour, baking powder, cinnamon, and nutmeg. Mix sifted mixture into raisin mixture. Fold in nuts. Drop by teaspoonfuls onto a greased cookie sheet. Bake at 375 degrees for 10 minutes.

Date Bars

½ pound dates, chopped
½ cup honey
¼ cup water
1 cup rolled oats
1 cup flour

¼ teaspoon salt
½ cup honey
½ cup butter, melted
½ teaspoon cinnamon

In a saucepan, combine dates, ½ cup honey, and water and cook over medium-low heat until thick. Cool. In a mixing bowl, blend oats, flour, salt, ½ cup honey, butter, and cinnamon. Spread half of the oat mixture in the bottom of a greased 8 x 8-inch pan. Cover with date mixture and top with remaining oat mixture. Bake at 350 degrees for 25 to 30 minutes.

Peanut Butter Fingers

1⅛ cups butter, softened
1⅛ cups sugar
1¼ cups brown sugar
¾ cup peanut butter
2 eggs

1½ teaspoons vanilla
2¼ cups flour
½ teaspoon baking soda
2¼ cups oatmeal

In a large mixing bowl, cream butter, sugars, and peanut butter. Add eggs and vanilla, mixing well. Mix in flour, baking soda, and oatmeal. Pour into a greased 9 x 13-inch pan and bake at 350 degrees for 18 to 20 minutes. Frost with recipe on page 140.

Frosting

⅜ cup milk
¼ cup peanut butter
2 cups powdered sugar

1½ teaspoons vanilla
¼ cup cocoa powder

In a saucepan, heat milk and peanut butter over low heat until peanut butter is dissolved. Add powdered sugar, vanilla, and cocoa powder. Spread on cooled bars. Cut into long, thin bars.

Cinnamon Candy

2 cups sugar
½ cup light corn syrup
½ cup boiling water

Dash of salt
2 to 3 drops cinnamon oil
Red food coloring

In a large saucepan, cook sugar, corn syrup, boiling water, and salt to hard crack stage without stirring. Remove from heat and sprinkle in cinnamon oil and food coloring. Rock the pan to mix. Pour into a greased 8 x 8-inch pan. Cut when candy is set but still warm.

French Cream Bar

3 pounds sugar
2 cups corn syrup
1 cup whipping cream
1 pound walnuts,
    coarsely chopped

1 pound Brazil nuts,
    coarsely chopped
1 pound dates, coarsely
    chopped

In a saucepan, cook sugar, corn syrup, and cream together until syrup forms a soft ball. Stir until cool. Add walnuts, Brazil nuts, and dates. Pack mixture into a greased loaf pan or shape into a roll using foil. Slice as needed. Candy will keep several weeks.

Molasses Taffy

2 cups molasses   Butter

Boil the molasses until it reaches hard ball stage (drop some in a cup of cold water and it should form a hard ball). Cool molasses in the pot until cool enough to be handled. Spread butter on hands and start by pulling the mass of molasses into a long strand. Fold the strand in half, bringing the two ends together. Twist the halves together like a rope. Have another person butter their hands and help. Pull each end of the taffy to stretch it, then repeat the fold and twist. Stretch, fold, and twist again until the taffy turns a cream color. Stretch the taffy into a rope, cut off 2-inch pieces with scissors, and wrap each piece in waxed paper.

Peanut Brittle

½ cup water
2 cups sugar
1 cup light corn syrup
2 cups raw peanuts

2 tablespoons butter
2 teaspoons baking soda
1 teaspoon vanilla

Grease 2 large cookie sheets. In a large saucepan, bring water to a boil; add sugar and corn syrup. Stir until dissolved. Boil until it will spin a thread. Add raw peanuts. Cook over low heat until mixture turns golden brown. Remove from heat. Add butter, baking soda, and vanilla. Stir quickly. Spread on cookie sheets. Place in cold area.

Peanut Candy

½ cup creamy peanut butter
½ cup honey
1 cup dry powdered milk

¾ cup peanut meal
(finely crushed nuts)

In a small bowl, combine peanut butter, honey, and powdered milk. Roll mixture into small balls and roll in nut meal to coat. Chill.

Pioneer Fruit

1 pound raisins
½ pound figs
½ pound dates
1 cup prunes

Juice and whole rind
   of 1 orange
1 cup pecans or walnuts,
   broken

Grind together fruits and orange rind. Mix well with orange juice and nuts. Shape into balls or flat bars. Place on a waxed paper-lined baking sheet and leave at room temperature for 24 hours in order to "ripen" before eating. You may choose to dip the candies in melted milk chocolate for added flair.

Our hearts grow tender with childhood memories and love of kindred, and we are better throughout the year for having, in spirit, become a child again at Christmastime.

LAURA INGALLS WILDER

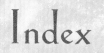

Index

Munchers and Sippers

Bacon Cheese Spread...8
Barbecue Bites..9
Black-Eyed Pea Dip..10
Caramel Corn...16
Cheddar Stuffed Mushrooms..11
Chestnuts and Bacon..12
Christmas Tea..19
Dried Beef Ball..13
Eggnog...23
Frothy Chocolate...24
Hanky Pankies..14
Hot Cranberry Punch..20

Kettle Corn 17
Oat Snack Mix. 18
Party Punch 21
Sauerkraut Balls. 15
Wassail. 22

Bread

Baking Powder Biscuits. 27
Cottage Cheese and Nut Bread 31
Date Nut Bread. 36
Hominy Bread 32
Honey Apple Raisin Nut Bread 37

Marmalade Bread 33
Poppy Seed Bread 38
Pumpkin Bread.. 34
Pumpkin Cornbread.. 35
Pumpkin Muffins.. 30
Refrigerator Rolls... 28
Rich Egg Rolls 29

Breakfast

Apple Cider Syrup 44
Apple Pancakes... 43
Bacon Gravy 55

Baked Millet Cereal 50
Baked Oatmeal 51
Breakfast Casserole 47
Cinnamon Coffee Cake 42
Cinnamon Sticky Buns 41
Cornmeal Mush 48
Creamed Eggs and Biscuits 52
Deluxe Grits 49
Dutch Honey 46
Sausage Balls 54
Scotch Eggs 53
Swedish Oven Pancakes 45

Meats and Main Dishes

Barbecued Chipped Ham 58
Black-Eyed Peas and Ham 59
Chestnut and Butternut Squash Soup 74
Day After Casserole 69
Giblet Gravy 67
Ham-Cranberry Loaf 61
Ham Balls 60
Ham and Turnip Bake 62
Home-Style Turkey 65
Hot Chicken Salad 70
Huntington Chicken 63
Lamb Stew 64

Lentil Pottage 75
Peanut Butter Soup.. 76
Pheasant with Wild Rice Stuffing 72
Savory Crock-Pot Turkey.. 66
Split Pea Soup.. 77
Supreme Baked Macaroni and Cheese 73
Turkey Bone Soup.. 78
Turkey Rice Casserole 68
Venison Roast 71

Vegetables, Sides, and Salads

Acorn Squash Rings 81

Amish Dressing 93
Amish Turnips 83
Apple-Cabbage Slaw 97
Apple Tree Salad 98
Baked Corn 84
Baked Yams and Apples.. 85
Carrot Salad.. 99
Chestnut Turkey Stuffing.. 94
Christmas Salad... 100
Cinnamon Cherry Salad.. 101
Cranberry Salad... 102
Cranberry and Walnut Coleslaw.. 103
Gingered Spaghetti Squash.. 86
Honey-Ginger Carrots.. 87

Maple-Glazed Parsnips..88
Noodles...96
Potato Bake...89
Ribbon Salad...104
Sauerkraut Salad...105
Sausage-Cornbread Dressing.......................................95
Sloppy Potatoes...90
Stewed Tomatoes...92
Stuffed Acorn Squash..82
Sweet Potato Casserole..91

Cakes, Desserts, and Pie

Apple Betty 112

Beet Cake 108

Brownie Pudding 114

Brown Sugar Pie 123

Butternut Squash Pie 124

Caramel Dumplings 113

Chocolate Kraut Cake 109

Date Pudding 115

Eggnog Pie 125

Fried Apples with Nuts 122

Gingerbread 111

Indian Pudding 116

Mock Pecan Pie 126
Old-Fashioned Mincemeat 119
Ozark Pudding 117
Pumpkin Crunch 120
Pumpkin Dessert 121
Rice Pudding 118
Root Beer Cake 110

Cookies and Candies

Bessie's Sugar Cookies 129
Butter Icing 135
Cherry Nut Cookies 130

Chocolate Cookies...131
Chocolate Cottage Cheese Cookies 132
Cinnamon Candy 141
Date Bars 138
Date Nut Pinwheels...133
French Cream Bar..142
Frosted Drop Cookies 134
Frosting 140
Maple Nut Cookies 136
Molasses Taffy...143
Peanut Candy 145
Peanut Brittle 144
Peanut Butter Fingers 139
Pioneer Fruit 146
Raisin Nut Drops 137